A Note From Rick Renner

I am on a personal quest to see a "revival of the Bible" so people can establish their lives on a firm foundation that will stand strong and endure the test as end-time storm winds begin to intensify.

In order to experience a revival of the Bible in your personal life, it is important to take time each day to read, receive, and apply its truths to your life. James tells us that if we will continue in the perfect law of liberty — refusing to be forgetful hearers, but determined to be doers — we will be blessed in our ways. As you watch or listen to the programs in this series and work through this corresponding study guide, I trust you will search the Scriptures and allow the Holy Spirit to help you hear something new from God's Word that applies specifically to your life. I encourage you to be a doer of the Word He reveals to you. Whatever the cost, I assure you — it will be worth it.

> Thy words were found, and I did eat them;
> and thy word was unto me the joy and rejoicing of mine heart:
> for I am called by thy name, O Lord God of hosts.
> — Jeremiah 15:16

Your brother and friend in Jesus Christ,

Rick Renner

Taming the Tongue & Discerning the Real Source of Revelations

Copyright © 2021 by Rick Renner
P.O. Box 702040
Tulsa, OK 74170

Published by Rick Renner Ministries
www.renner.org

ISBN 13: 978-1-68031-990-3

eBook ISBN 13: 978-1-68031-991-0

How To Use This Study Guide

This five-lesson study guide corresponds to *"Taming the Tongue and Discerning the Real Source of Revelations" With Rick Renner* (Renner TV). Each lesson in this study guide covers a topic that is addressed during the program series, with questions and references supplied to draw you deeper into your own private study of the Scriptures on this subject.

To derive the most benefit from this study guide, consider the following:

First, watch or listen to the program prior to working through the corresponding lesson in this guide. (Programs can also be viewed at **renner.org** by clicking on the Media/Archives links.)

Second, take the time to look up the scriptures included in each lesson. Prayerfully consider their application to your own life.

Third, use a journal or notebook to make note of your answers to each lesson's Study Questions and Practical Application challenges.

Fourth, invest specific time in prayer and in the Word of God to consult with the Holy Spirit. Write down the scriptures or insights He reveals to you.

Finally, take action! Whatever the Lord tells you to do according to His Word, do it.

For added insights on this subject, it is recommended that you obtain Rick Renner's books *Testing the Supernatural: How To Biblically Test Dreams, Visions, Revelations, and Spiritual Manifestations* and *How To Keep Your Head on Straight in a World Gone Crazy: Developing Discernment for These Last Days.* You may also select from Rick's other available resources by placing your order at **renner.org** or by calling 1-800-742-5593.

TOPIC
Be Careful What You Claim

SCRIPTURES

1. James 3:1 — My brethren, be not many masters, knowing that we shall receive the greater condemnation.
2. 1 Timothy 1:7 — Desiring to be teachers of the law; understanding neither what they say, nor whereof they affirm.

GREEK WORDS

1. "brethren" — ἀδελφός (*adelphos*): a term used to describe two or more who were born from the same womb; an endearing term used to describe those of one's own family; later used in a military sense to depict brothers in battle; a comrade; hence, brotherhood
2. "be" — γίνεσθε (*ginesthe*): be not in the process; be not becoming
3. "many" — πολλοὶ (*polloi*): numerous; substantial number
4. "masters" — διδάσκαλος (*didaskalos*): a teacher; intended to give the idea of one who is a fabulous, masterful teacher; the Greek equivalent for the Hebrew word rabbi; in a secular sense, it was used to describe a theatrical dramatic teacher who masterfully memorized and knew all the lines
5. "desiring" — θέλω (*thelo*): to long for; the tense depicts an earnest, ongoing, perpetual desire
6. "teachers of the law" — νομοδιδάσκαλος (*nomodidaskalos*): a word that only appears three times in the New Testament; a compound of the word νόμος (*nomos*) and διδάσκαλος (*didaskalos*); the word νόμος (*nomos*) means rules, principles, or the unchanging and unbendable rule of faith, and is where we get the word "law"; the word διδάσκαλος (*didaskalos*) refers to a masterful teacher; compounded, it pictures a scripture-lawyer or someone scholarly in interpreting the Bible
7. "understanding" — νοοῦντες (*noountes*): a form of nous, the word for the mind; this word refers to the ability to think, to reason, to understand, and to comprehend

8. "they say" — λέγουσιν (*legousin*): repeatedly say over and over
9. "affirm" — Διαβεβαιόομαι (*diabebaioomai*): to continuously assert, to continuously try to establish, to continuously affirm with confidence
10. "knowing" — οἶδα (*oida*): seeing; perceiving; understanding; comprehending; observing
11. "that" — ὅτι (*hoti*): pointing to a specific conclusion
12. "receive" — λαμβάνω (*lambano*): I grasp; I receive; I take; future tense, to grasp, to receive, to take
13. "greater" — μεῖζόν (*meidzon*): a form of μέγας (*megas*), but here greater comparatively to others
14. "condemnation" — κρίμα (*krima*): judgment; from κρίνω (*krino*), a word that usually referred to a jury who had just handed down their final sentence in a court of law; a verdict or a final sentence pronounced as the result of a court trial; after all the evidence had been presented and the judge had examined all the facts, a final verdict issued by the court

SYNOPSIS

The five lessons in this study on *Taming the Tongue and Discerning the Real Source of Revelations* will focus on the following topics:

- Be Careful What You Claim
- Taming the Tongue
- The Proof of Wisdom
- The Evidence of Wrong Revelation
- The Evidence of Right Revelation

The emphasis of this lesson:

No one should be too quick to claim to be a masterful teacher of Scripture. The Bible says those with spiritual influence who say they are masterful teachers of the Word will be scrutinized by God Himself and held to a higher standard than others.

James Called His Readers 'Brethren'

In the third chapter of the book of James, James continued his message of encouragement and correction to believers by saying, "My brethren, be not many masters, knowing that we shall receive the greater condemnation" (James 3:1).

As he had done many times in his letter, once again he addressed his readers as "brethren," which is the Greek word *adelphos*. It comes from the word *delphos*, the term for *a woman's womb*. When an "a" is attached to the front, it describes *two or more who were born from the same womb*. It is an endearing term used to describe those of one's own family.

James used this word repeatedly to connect with his readers. By calling them "brethren" (*adelphos*), he was saying, "You and I are born out of the same spiritual womb — the womb of God. Therefore, we are brothers and sisters." Likewise, James uses the word *adelphos* to denote a connection with his readers as fellow soldiers in God's army.

The word *adelphos* was first popularized by Alexander the Great, who was believed to be the greatest soldier living at that time. Consequently, every Greek soldier wanted to be affiliated with him in some way. So from time to time he would hold a huge ceremony to honor the warriors that had been in the trenches on the front lines slugging it out and giving it their very best. Alexander would stand on a stage and call out the names of the brave fighters one by one. When they came up and stood next to him, he would wrap his arm around them, and with his other arm he would wave at all the adoring soldiers and say, "Let all the empire know that Alexander the Great is proud to be the brother — *adelphos* — of this soldier."

Hence, this word carried the idea of *camaraderie* or a *brotherhood* of soldiers in the same fight. James and his readers were familiar with this word, and that is why he used it. The believers he wrote to were really struggling in their faith, but rather than condemn them for wavering, James called them "brethren," symbolically placing himself right down in the trenches next to them. The fact that these words came from James — the half-brother of Jesus — was powerfully encouraging to the hearers.

Every time he called them "brethren," it was like he wrapped his arm around them and said, "You and I are comrades in battle! You may be struggling in your faith, but you're still slugging it out and putting one foot in front of the other. And I want you and everyone else to know I'm proud to be your brother in Christ!" That's what this word *adelphos*, translated here as "brethren," means.

Don't Be Too Quick
To Call Yourself a Teacher

After his opening salutation, James went on to say, "…Be not many masters, knowing that we shall receive the greater condemnation" (James 3:1). Notice the first word "be." In Greek, it is the word *ginesthe*, which means *be not in the process* or *be not becoming.* The next word, "many," is the Greek word *polloi*, which means *numerous* or *a substantial number.*

This brings us to the word "masters" — the Greek word *didaskalos* — which describes *a teacher.* In this verse it is intended to give the idea of *one who is a fabulous, masterful teacher.* It is the Greek equivalent for the Hebrew word *rabbi*, and in a secular sense, it was used to describe a theatrical dramatic teacher who masterfully memorized and knew all the lines and the movements that were to be played out on the stage.

During the First Century, many believers wanted to be Bible teachers. In context here, James used this word *didaskalos* — "masters" — to caution his readers not to go about claiming to be masterful teachers, "…knowing that [teachers] shall receive the greater condemnation" (James 3:1).

Many Ephesian Believers
Were Longing To Be Teachers

The aspiration to be a teacher of the Word was apparently also an issue in the church at Ephesus where Timothy was the presiding pastor. In an effort to address this, Paul wrote to his young apprentice and said these believers were "desiring to be teachers of the law; [but] understanding neither what they say, nor whereof they affirm" (1 Timothy 1:7).

In a sense, Paul was both complimenting the believers and at the same time scolding them for wanting to be teachers. That is what the word "desiring" indicates. In Greek, it is the word *thelo*, and it means *to long for.* The tense here depicts *an earnest, ongoing, perpetual desire.* Hence, a number of the Ephesian believers were *longing* to be "teachers of the law."

This phrase "teachers of the law" in Greek is *nomodidaskalos*, a word that only appears three times in the New Testament. It's a compound of the words *nomos* and *didaskalos.* The word *nomos* depicts *rules, principles*, or *the unchanging, unbending rule of faith.* It is where we get the word *law.* And the word *didaskalos*, the same word we saw in James 3:1, refers to *a masterful teacher.* When these words are compounded to form *nomodidas-kalos*, it pictures *a scripture-lawyer* or *someone scholarly in interpreting the Bible.*

Apparently in Ephesus, there were a number of people who claimed to have a masterful grip on the Word of God, and, therefore, considered themselves authorized to teach like a Scripture lawyer. As it turns out, they were actually unqualified individuals boasting of being something that they were not.

They Spoke With Great Authority But Were Incorrect in What They Said

Paul said they were "…understanding neither what they say, nor whereof they affirm" (1 Timothy 1:7). The word "understanding" in Greek is *noountes*, a form of the word *nous*, which is the word for *the mind.* Here it refers to *the ability to think, to reason, to understand, and to comprehend.* These believers who were claiming to be masterful teachers were actually unable to think, reason, or comprehend "what they say."

The words "they say" is a translation of the Greek word *legousin*, which means *to repeatedly say over and over.* Paul's inclusion of this word indicates that these want-to-be teachers were repeating the same wrong teaching again and again. They were also clueless "whereof they affirm." The word "affirm" in Greek is *diabebaioomai*, which means *to continuously assert, to continuously try to establish,* or *to continuously affirm with confidence.* Hence, these individuals were speaking with great authority, but they were incorrect in what they were saying.

Paul was not questioning their desire or longing to be a Scripture lawyer. He was merely pointing out the fact that they were not ready for such a position. They lacked "understanding" (*noountes*), which means they weren't able to put together all the spiritual puzzle pieces and see the big picture. Thus, they were trying to function in a position they weren't qualified for.

Many times people make tragic doctrinal mistakes because they're incorrectly building an entire doctrine out of one or two obscure verses. They handle the Bible as if they are a Scripture lawyer, but what they repeatedly proclaim and affirm to be true is incorrect because it doesn't fit with the rest of God's Word.

Teachers of God's Word
Will Be More Closely Scrutinized

Returning once more to James 3:1, it says, "My brethren, be not many masters, knowing that we shall receive the greater condemnation" (James 3:1). The word "knowing" is a form of the Greek word *oida*, which here means *seeing, perceiving, understanding, comprehending,* or *observing.* And the word "that" is the Greek word *hoti,* which is a pointer word *pointing to something very important.*

The use of these two words indicates that James' readers had personally observed what happens to people who claim to be something they are not. In this verse, he was reminding them of what they had already seen. It's as if he was saying, "You've seen this for yourselves, and you can comprehend what I'm telling you is right. Those who claim to be masterful teachers of Scripture shall receive the greater condemnation."

The word "receive" is the familiar Greek word *lambano,* which means *I grasp; I receive; I take.* Here it is a future tense, indicating that those who claim to be masterful teachers *will grasp, will receive,* and *will take* "the greater condemnation." In Greek, the word "greater" is *meidzon,* a form of the word *megas,* but here it describes something *greater in comparison to others.*

The word "condemnation" is the Greek word *krima,* which describes *judgment.* It is from the Greek word *krino,* a word that usually referred to *a jury who had just handed down their final sentence in a court of law.* It is *a verdict or a final sentence pronounced as the result of a court trial.* After all the evidence has been presented and the judge has examined all the facts, a final verdict is issued by the court. That is what the word "condemnation" means.

In this verse, the Holy Spirit forewarns that those with spiritual influence — those who claim to be masterful teachers — will be scrutinized by God Himself. He will watch to see if what they endorse or teach is in agreement with the entire body of Scripture. That means every word, every phrase, and every nuance that is spoken in a public forum by a spiritual leader is significant to God.

Christian leaders must always remember that *words have consequences.* And according to James 3:1, those with spiritual influence over others will be held accountable for what they say, what they endorse, and what they serve to saints who are gathered at their table.

In our next lesson, we will turn our attention to the power of the tongue and how we are to tame it.

STUDY QUESTIONS

> Study to shew thyself approved unto God, a workman that needeth not to be ashamed, rightly dividing the word of truth.
> — 2 Timothy 2:15

1. Just as every word, every phrase, and every nuance that is spoken in a public forum by a spiritual leader is significant to God, the words you speak are also very important. What did Jesus say about your words in Matthew 12:36,37? (Also consider Proverbs 10:19 and 29:11.)

2. Desiring to be a spiritual leader is certainly honorable and commendable. At the same time, it is a position that God scrutinizes more closely. Take a few moments to identify some of what God requires of those who lead His Church in these passages:

    - Titus 1:6-9

    - 2 Timothy 2:14-26

    - 2 Timothy 3:14-17 and 4:1-5

    What is the Holy Spirit speaking to you personally in these passages?

PRACTICAL APPLICATION

> But be ye doers of the word, and not hearers only, deceiving your own selves.
> — James 1:22

1. Again and again throughout James' letter, he called his readers 'brethren," placing himself side by side in the trenches as a fellow soldier fighting together against the enemy. What seasoned saint has God used to encourage you in your Christian walk? What did they say or do to give you hope and strength to stay in the game and keep fighting?

2. What fellow believer do you know that could use some encouragement right now? Why not reach out to them by phone, by mail, or

by text and let them know how proud you are to be their comrade. Celebrate them for still being in the fight and pray for the Holy Spirit to strengthen them to continue standing against the enemy.

3. There were a number of believers in the church of Ephesus who were longing to be masterful teachers of Scripture, but they were actually unqualified to operate in that role. Have you ever observed someone who was unqualified to do a particular job? What was the result of their unpreparedness? Why do you think it's so important to really have a grasp on a biblical subject before one begins teaching it?

4. According to James 3:1, those who claim to be masterful teachers will be scrutinized by God Himself. Every word, every phrase, and every nuance that is spoken in a public forum by a spiritual leader is significant to God, because words have consequences and affect others. How does this spiritual truth challenge you personally?

LESSON 2

TOPIC

Taming the Tongue

SCRIPTURES

1. James 3:2-12 — For in many things we offend all. If any man offend not in word, the same is a perfect man, and able also to bridle the whole body. Behold, we put bits in the horses' mouths, that they may obey us; and we turn about their whole body. Behold also the ships, which though they be so great, and are driven of fierce winds, yet are they turned about with a very small helm, whithersoever the governor listeth. Even so the tongue is a little member, and boasteth great things. Behold, how great a matter a little fire kindleth! And the tongue is a fire, a world of iniquity: so is the tongue among our members, that it defileth the whole body, and setteth on fire the course of nature; and it is set on fire of hell. For every kind of beasts, and of birds, and of serpents, and of things in the sea, is tamed, and hath been tamed of mankind: But the tongue can no man tame; it is an unruly evil, full of deadly poison. Therewith bless we God, even the Father; and therewith curse we men, which are made after the simili-

tude of God. Out of the same mouth proceedeth blessing and cursing. My brethren, these things ought not so to be. Doth a fountain send forth at the same place sweet water and bitter? Can the fig tree, my brethren, bear olive berries? either a vine, figs? so can no fountain both yield salt water and fresh.

GREEK WORDS

1. "offend" — πταίω (*ptaio*): to stumble; to err; to mess up
2. "in word" — ἐν λόγῳ (*en logo*): in what he says or speaks
3. "the same" — οὗτος (*houtos*): this very one
4. "perfect man" — τέλειος (*teleios*): a full-grown adult; pictures the process of transitioning from being youthful and immature to an individual who is full-grown and mature; in the New Testament it denotes spiritually mature individuals
5. "able" — δυνατός (*dunatos*): from δύναμις (*dunamis*), which is power or ability; depicts the assembled forces of an army whose combined strength enabled them to achieve unrivaled victories; these troops were so strong that they could not be resisted; to have ability, power, or strength; to be able
6. "bridle" — χαλιναγωγέω (*chalinagogeo*): to bridle; to hold in check; to restrain; to control
7. "whole body" — ὅλον τὸ σῶμα (*holon to soma*): their whole or entire body; direction is determined by the mouth
8. "bits" — χαλινός (*chalinos*): a bridle; a bit
9. "obey" — πείθω (*peitho*): to sway from one direction to go in a different direction
10. "turn about" — μετάγω (*metago*): to lead differently; to turn about; to change direction
11. "behold" — ἰδού (*idou*): bewilderment, shock, amazement, and wonder
12. "also" — καί (*kai*): additionally
13. "ships" — πλοῖον (*ploion*): large ships
14. "so great" — τηλικοῦτος (*telikoutos*): great in size; huge; vast; powerful in size and ability
15. "driven" — ἐλαύνω (*elauno*): to drive; push; force
16. "of" — ὑπὸ (*hupo*): directly by
17. "fierce" — σκληρός (*skleros*): harsh, stern, rough, violent

18. "winds" — **ἄνεμος** (*anemos*): storm-like forces
19. "turned about" — **μετάγω** (*metago*): to lead differently; to turn about; to change direction
20. "with" — **ὑπὸ** (*hupo*): directly by
21. "very small helm" — **ἐλαχίστου πηδαλίου** (*elaxhistou pedaliou*): a small, little rudder
22. "withersoever the governor listeth" — **ὅπου ἡ ὁρμὴ τοῦ εὐθύνοντος βούλεται** (*hopou he horme tou euthunontos bouletai*): wherever the one steering resolves to go; meaning the ship is directed by the one controlling the rudder
23. "even so" — **οὕτως καὶ** (*houtos kai*): likewise also; likewise additionally; in the very same way
24. "the tongue" — **ἡ γλῶσσα** (*he glossa*): with a definite article, THE tongue
25. "little" — **μικρός** (*mikros*): very little; tiny; where we get the word micro or microscopic
26. "member" — **μέλος** (*melos*): member; organ of the body; used in antiquity to depict part of a ship needed to move the ship along; also used to depict weapons of war
27. "boasteth great things" — **μεγάλα αὐχεῖ** (*megala auchei*): to make a big commotion or noise
28. "behold" — **ἰδού** (*idou*): bewilderment, shock, amazement, and wonder
29. "a little fire" — **ἡλίκον πῦρ** (*helikon pur*): a small fire

SYNOPSIS

How would you like to be able to control your entire body? According to James, it is possible. In fact, he said the one who can control his body is a *perfect man* — one who is spiritually mature and can be entrusted with adult responsibilities.

Interestingly, the connection between spiritual maturity and control over one's body is directly linked to the mastery of one's mouth. Indeed, "Death and life are in the power of the tongue..." (Proverbs 18:21). That includes *your* tongue. As you learn to harness the power of your words to produce life, the greater God's power becomes in and through your life.

The emphasis of this lesson:

Controlling what you say is a sign of spiritual maturity. It produces great power, giving you the ability to control your entire body. Like a small bit in a horse's mouth or the tiny rudder on a ship, the tongue gives direction to your life. Only a tongue surrendered to the Holy Spirit can be tamed and avoid bringing death and destruction to the lives of others.

Controlling What You Say Releases Power and Is a Sign of Spiritual Maturity

When we come to James 3:2, the Holy Spirit begins to zero in on an area in everyone's life where growth and maturity are needed — the area of the *mouth*. James writes, "For in many things we offend all. If any man offend not in word, the same is a perfect man, and able also to bridle the whole body."

The word "offend" here could have been a number of different Greek words. However, in this verse it is the word *patio*, which simply means *to stumble; to err;* or *to mess up.* Thus, James said, "For in many things *we all mess up and make mistakes.* But if any man doesn't *stumble or err* in word, the same is a perfect man...."

In Greek, the phrase "in word" is *en logo,* which means *in what he says or speaks,* and the words "the same" are a translation of the Greek word *houtos,* meaning *this very one.* Hence, when a person doesn't make mistakes in what he says or speaks, the Bible says he is a "perfect man." This phrase is a form of the Greek word *teleios,* which describes *a full-grown adult.* It pictures *the process of transitioning from being youthful and immature to an individual who is full-grown and mature.* In the New Testament, the word *teleios* denotes spiritually mature individuals who can be entrusted with adult responsibilities.

James says the mature, grown-up believer is "...able also to bridle the whole body" (James 3:2). The word "able" is the Greek word *dunatos,* from the word *dunamis,* which is *power, strength,* or *ability.* It depicts *the assembled forces of an army whose combined strength enabled them to achieve unrivaled victories.* These troops were so strong that they could not be resisted. The word *dunamis* also denoted *a force of nature,* such as a hurricane, a tornado, or an earthquake.

Thus, when a person can control his mouth, he has supernatural ability and power. Like a mighty Roman army, he can forcefully take ground away from his enemy. In fact, he is so strong he can "bridle the whole body." The word "bridle" is the Greek word *chalinagogeo*, which is the term for *a horse's bridle* and means *to bridle; to hold in check; to restrain;* or *to control*. And the phrase "whole body" in Greek is *holon to soma*, describing *the whole or entire body*. A person who is able to control his mouth and not let it say just anything it wants is a person with great power.

The Strength and Direction
Of a Horse Is Controlled Through Its Mouth

James expanded his analogy of the horse and how it's controlled in verse 3, saying, "Behold, we put bits in the horses' mouths, that they may obey us; and we turn about their whole body" (James 3:3). The word "Behold" here in Greek is like an exclamation declaring, "Wow! This is amazing!"

If you stop and think about what James said, it *is* truly amazing. Horses are huge, powerful animals. The fact that a small "bit" — the Greek word *chalino* — in their mouth can direct and control their energy and efforts is simply remarkable! If you have control over the horse's mouth, you have control over the whole horse.

James said controlling the horse's mouth causes them to "…obey us; and we turn about their whole body" (James 3:3)." The word "obey" in Greek is *peitho*, which means *to sway from one direction to go in a different direction*. The phrase "turn about" is from the Greek word *metago*, meaning *to lead differently; to turn about;* or *to change direction*. And the words "whole body" are a translation of the Greek words *holon to soma*, which again describes *their whole or entire body*.

Essentially, James is telling us that if we control our mouth, we can control everything about us and turn our lives — and keep them turned — in the right direction.

Huge Ships Are Steered
and Directed by a Small Rudder

To make sure we understood, James followed up with another analogy in the next verse, saying, "Behold also the ships, which though they be so great, and are driven of fierce winds, yet are they turned about with a very small helm, whithersoever the governor listeth" (James 3:4).

Again, he included the word "behold" — the Greek word *idou* — describing *bewilderment, shock, amazement,* and *wonder.* It is the equivalent of him saying, "Wow! This is shocking and amazing!" Then he wrote about the power of "ships," which is the Greek word *ploion,* the word for *large ships* that are "so great." This description is taken from the Greek word *telikoutos,* meaning *great in size; huge; vast;* or *powerful in size and ability.*

James said these enormous ships "are driven of fierce winds." The word "driven" in Greek is *elauno,* which means *to drive, push,* or *force.* The word "of" is the Greek word *hupo,* meaning *directly by,* and the word "fierce" is the Greek word *skleros,* describing something *harsh, stern, rough,* or *violent.* Hence, these mighty, enormous ships were driven and pushed directly by harsh and violent "winds," which in Greek signifies *storm-like forces.*

In spite of their tremendous size and the rough storm-like forces coming against them, James said, "…Yet are they [the ships] turned about with a very small helm…" (James 3:4). The phrase "turned about" is again the Greek word *metago,* which means *to lead differently; to turn about;* or *to change direction.* The word "with" is the Greek word *hupo,* which means *directly by,* and the phrase "very small helm" in Greek describes *a small, little rudder.*

Just like a small bit in a horse's mouth moves him where he needs to go, a small rudder on a huge ship leads it in the direction "withersoever the governor listeth." In Greek, this phrase means *wherever the one steering resolves to go.* In other words, the ship is directed by the one controlling the rudder. Interestingly, this principle holds true for a fishing boat three yards in length or an aircraft carrier that is three football fields in length. Likewise, it holds true for the human tongue. The one who controls his tongue will also direct the course of his life.

Though the Tongue Is Tiny, It Is Incredibly Powerful

After comparing our tongue to small bits in the mouths' of horses and small rudders on enormous ships, James added, "Even so the tongue is a little member, and boasteth great things. Behold, how great a matter a little fire kindleth!" (James 3:5)

The opening words "even so" in Greek are *houtos kai*, meaning *likewise also*; *likewise additionally*, or *in the very same way*. "The tongue" in Greek is *he glossa*, which includes a definite article, meaning *THE tongue*. It is almost as if James is raising his voice and emphatically saying, "*THE tongue* is the real issue, even though it is a little member...."

The word "little" here is the Greek word *mikros*, meaning *very little* or *tiny*. It's from where we get the word *micro* or *microscopic*. The word "member" in Greek is *melos*, which describes *a member* or *an organ of the body*. This word was used in antiquity to depict the *part of a ship needed to move the ship along*. Curiously, it was also used to depict *weapons of war*, which means while the tongue can produce movement in the right direction, it can also say things that release destruction and lead us into war with others.

James said the tongue "boasteth great things." This phrase is a translation of the Greek words *megala auchei*, meaning *to make a big commotion or noise*. James immediately followed this statement with the words, "...Behold, how great a matter a little fire kindleth!" (James 3:5) Once again, we see James was overtaken with a sense of *bewilderment*, *shock*, and *wonder*, which is why he used the word "Behold" — the Greek word *idou*.

The Tongue Is a 'World of Iniquity'

James elaborated further in verse 6: "And the tongue is a fire, a world of iniquity: so is the tongue among our members, that it defileth the whole body, and setteth on fire the course of nature; and it is set on fire of hell" (James 3:6).

Notice the phrase "a world of iniquity." In Greek, it is *ho kosmos tes adikias*, and it means *a universe or its own world, filled with hurt, injustice, wickedness, and violations*. That is what the tongue is — a world of its own that is filled with hurt, injustice, wickedness, and violations.

Furthermore, James said that the tongue "defileth." This is the Greek word *spilos*, which is from where we get the word *spill*. It means *to stain, defile, or to contaminate*. It carries the idea of *spilling something that creates a permanent stain, permanent defilement*, or *permanent contamination*. That is what the tongue is capable of doing.

The reason for its potential destruction is because it is "…set on fire of hell" (James 3:6). The Greek here literally says, *being ignited and inflamed by hell itself.*"

No Man Can Tame the Tongue

James goes on to say, "For every kind of beasts, and of birds, and of serpents, and of things in the sea, is tamed, and hath been tamed of mankind" (James 3:7). The word "beasts" in Greek describes *wild, ferocious animals that are difficult to tame*, such as lions, tigers, and bears. To this list, he also adds birds, serpents, and things in the sea. Although all these animals are very hard to train, it can be done. James says each of these animals "…is tamed, and hath been tamed of mankind" (James 3:7).

The word "tamed" is the Greek word *damadzo*, which means *to domesticate, to subdue, or to bring under control*. This word was used to describe *animal trainers who were experts at capturing and domesticating the wildest and most ferocious of beasts*, such as lions, tigers, and bears. All these beasts and birds, serpents and sea creatures are tamable. "But the tongue can no man tame; it is an unruly evil, full of deadly poison" (James 3:8).

The opening word "but" is the Greek word *de*, which means *however, categorically*; or *emphatically*. It is like an exclamation to grab our attention as it points to "the tongue," which is again the Greek words *ten glossan*. It includes a definite article, THE tongue. In contrast to all the animals James has already named that can be tamed, he said, "…*THE tongue* can no man tame…" (James 3:8).

In Greek, "no man" indicates *absolutely no one*. The word "tame" is again the Greek word *damadzo*, meaning *to domesticate, to subdue, or to bring under control*. Hence, absolutely no one can domesticate, subdue, or bring under control his own tongue.

The Tongue Is an Unruly Evil and Full of Deadly Poison

The reason the tongue is untamable is because it is "…an unruly evil, full of deadly poison" (James 3:8). The word "unruly" is the Greek word *akatastatos*, which describes *something unstable, restless, or uncontrollable*. It is actually the very word for *an anarchist*, which tells us that *anarchy* resides in the tongue. Anarchy and war begin with words, and words are formed by the tongue.

Moreover, James said this unruliness is "evil," which is the Greek word *kakos*, depicting *words that are bad or inappropriate*. Not only is the tongue ripe with unruly evil, but it is also "full of deadly poison." The word "full" here is the Greek word *mestos*, meaning *full* or *loaded*. The phrase "deadly poison" is a form of the Greek word *thanatephoros*, which literally means *death-producing*. This word was used by Greek writers to depict *arrows or words that carried death*. Like venom carried by poisonous snakes, the tongue is an instrument that is full of deadly poison.

Essentially, what James is saying here is that the untamed tongue will look for opportunities to shoot its arrows of death at others. Like a poisonous asp or viper, it is waiting to strike its next victim. It wants to press its fangs down deep and release its poisonous venom into them.

There's only one way your tongue can be tamed, and that is by surrendering it to the control of the Holy Spirit. If you do this and tame your tongue, you will abound in power and have the ability to control your whole body!

STUDY QUESTIONS

Study to shew thyself approved unto God, a workman that needeth not to be ashamed, rightly dividing the word of truth.
— 2 Timothy 2:15

1. Take time to reflect on James 3:3,4. How do the examples of the bit in a horse's mouth and the rudder of a ship help you better understand the power of your tongue? What new insights is the Holy Spirit showing you about your tongue's ability to direct your life?

2. James 3:8 says that no man or woman can tame the tongue. Although at face value the situation seems hopeless, it is not. Why? Look at what the Bible says in these verses for the answer: Matthew 19:26; Mark 10:27; Luke 1:37 and 18:27.

3. The Bible has much to say about the words you speak. Take a few moments to look up and meditate on the meaning of these words of wisdom.

- How might you summarize Proverbs 18:20,21 in modern-day lingo?
- What do Proverbs 13:3 and 21:23 say about guarding what you say?
- According to Psalm 34:11-13 and First Peter 3:9-11, watching your words is directly linked to what vital virtue? When you learn to cooperate with the Holy Spirit and guard your mouth, what blessings can you expect?

PRACTICAL APPLICATION

But be ye doers of the word, and not hearers only,
deceiving your own selves.
— James 1:22

1. According to James 3:2, the condition of your body reveals the health of your words. Be honest. What kind of shape is your body in? Are you strong and fit or overweight? Do you control your appetites, or do your appetites control you?

2. The tongue not only forms our words, but it is also the instrument with which we taste our food. Did you ever stop and think about the connection between our physical appetite and our tendency to give into temptation? Consider what Satan used to lure Eve into sin at the beginning of creation (*see* Genesis 3:1-7), along with Paul's words of warning in First Corinthians 6:12,13. How important do you think it is to surrender your taste buds and food cravings to the Holy Spirit?

LESSON 3

TOPIC

The Proof of Wisdom

SCRIPTURES

1. James 3:6-15 — And the tongue is a fire, a world of iniquity: so is the tongue among our members, that it defileth the whole body, and setteth on fire the course of nature; and it is set on fire of hell. For every kind of beasts, and of birds, and of serpents, and of things in

the sea, is tamed, and hath been tamed of mankind: But the tongue can no man tame; it is an unruly evil, full of deadly poison. Therewith bless we God, even the Father; and therewith curse we men, which are made after the similitude of God. Out of the same mouth proceedeth blessing and cursing. My brethren, these things ought not so to be. Doth a fountain send forth at the same place sweet water and bitter? Can the fig tree, my brethren, bear olive berries? either a vine, figs? so can no fountain both yield salt water and fresh. Who is a wise man and endued with knowledge among you? let him shew out of a good conversation his works with meekness of wisdom. But if ye have bitter envying and strife in your hearts, glory not, and lie not against the truth. This wisdom descendeth not from above, but is earthly, sensual, devilish.

GREEK WORDS

1. "the tongue is a fire" — ἡ γλῶσσα πῦρ (*he glossa pur*): with a definite article, THE tongue is fire

2. "a world of iniquity" — ὁ κόσμος τῆς ἀδικίας (*ho kosmos tes adikias*): a universe or its own world, filled with hurt, injustice, wickedness, and violations

3. "defileth" — σπῖλος (*spilos*): to stain, defile, or to contaminate; to spill something that creates a stain; permanent defilement; permanent contamination

4. "setteth on fire" — φλογίζω (*phlogidzo*): ignite; raging passions

5. "set on fire of hell" — καὶ φλογιζομένη ὑπὸ τῆς γεέννης (*kai phlougidzomene hupo tes geennes*): being ignited and inflamed by hell itself

6. "tamed" — δαμάζω (*damadzo*): to domesticate, to subdue, or to bring under control; used to describe animal trainers who were experts at capturing and domesticating the wildest and most ferocious of beasts, such as lions, tigers, and bears

7. "but" — δὲ (*de*): but; however; categorically; emphatically

8. "the tongue" — τὴν γλῶσσαν (*ten glossan*): with a definite article, THE tongue

9. "no man" — οὐδεὶς (*oudeis*): absolutely no one

10. "tame" — δαμάζω (*damadzo*): to domesticate, to subdue, or to bring under control

11. "unruly" — **ἀκατάστατος** (*akatastatos*): unstable; uncontrollable; anarchist
12. "evil" — **κακός** (*kakos*): depicts words that are bad or inappropriate
13. "full" — **μεστός** (*mestos*): full; loaded
14. "deadly poison" — **ἰοῦ θανατηφόρου** (*iou thanatephorou*): from **ἰός** (*ios*), the poison of asps; the word **θανατηφόρος** (*thanatephoros*) means death producing; used by Greek writers to depict arrows or words that carried death; here, words carry poison and death
15. "bless" — **εὐλογέω** (*eulogeo*): words that are good; blessings are verbally released
16. "curse" — **καταράομαι** (*kataraomai*): from **κατά** (*kata*) and **ἀρά** (*ara*); **κατά** (*kata*) means down, and **ἀρά** (*ara*) is a curse or incantation; to speak a curse down on something; to verbally doom
17. "mouth" — **στόμα** (*stoma*): physical mouth; used figuratively for the point of a sword
18. "fountain" — **πηγή** (*pege*): fountain, the mouth is a fountain for what is inside a person
19. "send forth" — **βρύω** (*bruo*): gush; to be gushing forth, like a strong flowing underground stream
20. "sweet water and bitter" — **τὸ γλυκὺ καὶ τὸ πικρόν** (*to gluku kai to pikron*): the word **γλυκύς** (*glukus*) means sweet, and **πικρός** (*pikros*) means acidic, bitter, distasteful, sharp, toxic
21. "shew" — **δείκνυμι** (*deiknumi*): something outwardly seen; something done visibly to authenticate, prove, or guarantee; to prove by showing; to display or show off; to demonstrate
22. "out of a good conversation" — **ἐκ τῆς καλῆς ἀναστροφῆς** (*ek tes kales anastrophes*): the word **ἐκ** (*ek*) means out, and **καλός** (*kalos*) means beautiful, noble, honorable, and **ἀναστροφή** (*anastrophe*) is one's lifestyle or his rising up and setting down, his going in and going out; out of a good manner of life; one's total life that is lived in a noble manner
23. "meekness" — **πραΰτης** (*prautes*): the demeanor of a person who is soothing medication for a troubled or angry mind
24. "wisdom" — **σοφία** (*sophia*): wisdom; revelation

SYNOPSIS

The Bible says, "Words satisfy the mind as much as fruit does the stomach; good talk is as gratifying as a good harvest. Words kill, words give life; they're either poison or fruit — you choose" (Proverbs 18:20,21 *MSG*).

James took these words to heart and spent most of the third chapter of his book teaching about the power of the tongue and how to discern right and wrong revelation. Although no man can tame his tongue, the Holy Spirit is able to tame it once it has been submitted to His sanctifying power. Indeed, he who controls the words of his mouth harnesses the power to direct his life.

The emphasis of this lesson:

The tongue is restless, unstable, and inflamed by hell itself. Like a poisonous snake, it is waiting to strike and release its toxin into its next victim. But if we submit our tongue to the Holy Spirit, He will turn our bitter words into sweet words and our curses into blessing. The one who has true wisdom from Heaven proves it by the words he speaks and the way he lives.

Teachers of the Word
Will Be Held to a Higher Standard

In our first lesson, we examined James 3:1, which says, "My brethren, be not many masters, knowing that we shall receive the greater condemnation." In this verse, James cautioned his readers not to be too quick to claim to be "masters," which is the word *didaskalos*, the Greek equivalent for the Hebrew word *Rabbi*. It describes *one who has a masterful grip on the Scriptures.*

This is the very same word often used in the four gospels by the disciples when they called Jesus "Master." They were acknowledging that He was the One with the most masterful grip on the Scriptures. The word *didaskalos* — translated here as "masters" — carries the idea of *a revelator.*

James said that those who claim to be masterful teachers of the Word "...shall receive the greater condemnation" (James 3:1). We saw that the word "condemnation" is the Greek word *krima*, which describes *judgment.* It is from the word *krino*, which usually referred to *a jury who had just handed down their final sentence in a court of law.* After all the evidence had been presented and the judge had examined all the facts, a final verdict was issued by the court.

In this verse, the Holy Spirit forewarns that those with spiritual influence — those who claim to be revelators or masterful teachers — will be scrutinized by God Himself. He will study to see if what they endorse or teach is in agreement with the entirety of Scripture. That means every word, every phrase, and every nuance that is spoken in a public forum by a spiritual leader is significant to God.

Christian leaders must always remember that *words have consequences*. And according to James 3:1, those with spiritual influence over others will be held accountable for what they say, what they endorse, and what they serve to those who are gathered at their table.

The Human Tongue Is Like a Horse's Bit and a Ship's Rudder

James went on to say, "For in many things we offend all. If any man offend not in word, the same is a perfect man, and able also to bridle the whole body" (James 3:2). We noted that the word "offend" here is the Greek word *ptaio*, which simply means *to stumble*, *to err*, or *to mess up*. Here, James was saying, "For in many things *we all mess up and make mistakes*. But if anyone doesn't *make mistakes in what he says*, he is a perfect man...."

A person who is able to control his mouth and not let it say just anything it wants is a person with great power and spiritual maturity. In other words, if you can tame your tongue, you can tame every other area of your life.

James then gave two specific examples of what the tongue is like. First, he said, "Behold, we put bits in the horses' mouths, that they may obey us; and we turn about their whole body" (James 3:3). Horses are huge, powerful animals, yet they can be directed and controlled by placing a small "bit" in their mouths!

The same thing is true of ships. James said, "Behold also the ships, which though they be so great, and are driven of fierce winds, yet are they turned about with a very small helm, whithersoever the governor listeth" (James 3:4). The Greek word for "ships" here is *ploion*, which describes *large ships* that are not only great in size, but massive in strength.

Even though these enormous ships are driven and pushed by fierce, storm-like winds, James said, "…Yet are they turned about with a very small helm…" (James 3:4). The phrase "turned about" is the Greek word *metago*, which means *to lead differently, to turn about*, or *to change direction*. The word "with" is the Greek word *hupo*, which means *directly by*, and the phrase "very small helm" in Greek describes *a small, little rudder*.

Just like a small bit in a horse's mouth moves him where he needs to go, a small rudder on a huge ship leads it in the direction in which the one steering decides to go. In other words, the ship is directed by the one controlling the rudder.

When we come to verse 5, James connected his examples to the tongue when he said, "Even so the tongue is a little member, and boasteth great things. Behold, how great a matter a little fire kindleth!" (James 3:5) The words "even so" in Greek are *houtos kai*, meaning *likewise also; likewise additionally*, or *in the very same way*. Just as the horse's bit and the ship's rudder are small but powerful, the tongue is a "little member" in comparison to the rest of the body.

This word "little" is the Greek word *mikros*, meaning *very little* or *tiny*. It's where we get the word *micro* or *microscopic*. The Greek word for "member" is *melos*, which describes *a member or an organ of the body*. This word was used in ancient times to depict the *rudder of a ship needed to move the ship along in the right direction*. It was also used by Greeks to depict *weapons of war*. This tells us that while the tongue may be small, if used correctly, it will keep you moving in the right direction. However, if used incorrectly, your tongue will become a weapon of war.

The Tongue Is Capable of Leaving a Permanent Stain

Just how bad can the tongue be? James began to tell us in verse 6: "And the tongue is a fire, a world of iniquity: so is the tongue among our members, that it defileth the whole body, and setteth on fire the course of nature; and it is set on fire of hell" (James 3:6). For a second time in this passage, we see James use a definite article to emphasize the real issue we're dealing with — THE tongue.

James called the tongue a fire and "a world of iniquity." In Greek, this phrase is *ho kosmos tes adikias*, which means *a universe or its own world, filled with hurt, injustice, wickedness, and violations.* That is what the tongue is — a universe of its own that is filled with hurt, injustice, wickedness, and all kinds of violations.

What's more, James said that the tongue "defileth the whole body." In Greek, the word "defileth" is a translation of the word *spilos*, which is where we get the word *spill*. It literally means *to stain, to defile*, or *to contaminate*. It carries the idea of *spilling something that creates a permanent stain, permanent defilement*, or *permanent contamination*.

Imagine someone is walking through your living room with a glass of grape juice, and you have white carpet. Suddenly, they trip and the juice goes all over the carpet. No matter how much you apply stain remover and scrub, the stain will not budge. Days, weeks, and months pass, and every time you see that grape juice on your white carpet, the stain reminds you of the person who foolishly carried a glass of grape juice while walking through your living room. The stain is a *permanent reminder.*

In the same way, we can use our tongue to speak negative, hurtful things to others or about others that become like a permanent stain. Those hurtful words defile (or stain) both the hearer and the one being talked about. Think about it. Have you ever heard someone malign or bash the character of someone else? Whether the words were true or not, they left a permanent mark on your thinking. That's what the word "defileth" means.

Once the body is defiled and contaminated by the tongue, the Bible says, "…[It] setteth on fire the course of nature; and is set on fire of hell" (James 3:6). The phrase "setteth on fire" is a translation of the Greek word *phlogidzo*, which means *to ignite*. It describes *raging passions that are burning out of control.* Indeed, the tongue "is set on fire of hell," which in the Greek literally means, *being ignited and inflamed by hell itself.*

Although Wild Beasts Can Be Tamed, the Tongue Is Untamable

James continued, saying, "For every kind of beasts, and of birds, and of serpents, and of things in the sea, is tamed, and hath been tamed of mankind" (James 3:7). The word "beasts" here is the Greek word *therion*, which describes *wild, ferocious animals that are difficult to tame*, such as lions, tigers, and bears. After beasts, James mentioned *birds.* They, too, can be trained to carry messages and even to speak. *Serpents* can also be tamed to do certain things. The same is true of "things in the sea," which refers to *marine creatures*, such as giant whales that are trained to jump out of the water and through hoops.

James said each of these animals "…is tamed, and hath been tamed of mankind" (James 3:7). This word "tamed" is the Greek word *damadzo*, which means *to domesticate, to subdue, or to bring under control*. It was used to describe *animal trainers who were experts at capturing and domesticating the wildest and most ferocious of beasts*, such as lions, tigers, and bears. All these beasts, birds, serpents, and sea creatures are tamable. "But the tongue can no man tame; it is an unruly evil, full of deadly poison" (James 3:8).

This first word "but" in verse 8 is the Greek word *de*, which means *however, categorically*, or *emphatically*. It is like an exclamation to grab our attention. The phrase "the tongue" is, again, the Greek words *ten glossan*, which includes a definite article — THE tongue. In contrast to all the animals James has already named that can be tamed, he said, "…*THE tongue* can no man tame…" (James 3:8).

In Greek, "no man" indicates *absolutely no one*. The word "tame" is again the Greek word *damadzo*, meaning *to domesticate, to subdue, or to bring under control*. Hence, absolutely no one can subdue his own tongue and bring it under control.

The Tongue Is an 'Unruly Evil, Full of Deadly Poison'

What else did James tell us about the tongue? He said it was "…an unruly evil, full of deadly poison" (James 3:8). In Greek, the word "unruly" is *akatastatos*, which denotes *something unstable, restless, or uncontrollable*. It's actually the very word for *an anarchist*, which means that *anarchy* resides in the tongue. Because the tongue is so unstable and restless, its behavior is almost impossible to predict.

Moreover, James describes this unruliness as "evil," which is the Greek word *kakos*, depicting *words that are bad or inappropriate*. In addition to being ripe with unruly evil, the tongue is also "…full of deadly poison" (James 3:8). The word "full" here is the Greek word *mestos*, which describes something *full, loaded*, or *jam-packed*. The word "poison" is the Greek word *ios*, which is literally *the poison of asps*, and it is "deadly," which means *death-producing.* In Greek, "deadly" is the word *thanatephoros*, and it was used by Greek writers to depict *arrows or words that carried death.*

Essentially, what James was saying here is that the untamed tongue — the tongue that is not submitted to the Holy Spirit — is like a poisonous snake just waiting to strike. Its poison banks are in its head, and the instant it bites, it presses its syringe-like fangs into its victim until all its death-producing poison is released. That is exactly what the human tongue will do if it is not surrendered to God.

The Tongue Can 'Bless' or 'Curse'

The stark comparison of the tongue's potential continues in James 3:9, "Therewith bless we God, even the Father; and therewith curse we men, which are made after the similitude of God." The word "bless" here is the Greek word *eulogeo*, which is a compound of the words *eu* and *logos*. The word *eu* describes *something good or wonderful,* and the word *logos* is the Greek term for *words.* When these two words are compounded to form *eulogeo,* it describes *words that are good* or *blessings that are verbally released.*

By definition, *blessings* are never silent; they are *good words that are verbally expressed.* Ephesians 1:3 says, "…[God] hath blessed us with all spiritual blessings in heavenly places in Christ." And because He has blessed us, we are able to bless Him and speak words of blessings to others.

Unfortunately, we can also use our mouth to curse others. The word "curse" in James 3:9 is the Greek word *kataraomai,* which is a compound of the words *kata* and *ara.* The word *kata* means *down,* and *ara* is the term for *a curse* or *an incantation.* When these words are joined, the new word *kataraomai* means *to speak a curse down on something or someone.* It is the action of *verbally dooming or damning someone.*

James went on to say, "Out of the same mouth proceedeth blessing and cursing. My brethren, these things ought not so to be" (James 3:10). Here in this verse, we see for the seventh time in his epistle, James addresses his readers as "brethren," the Greek word *adelphos.* In doing so, he places himself on their level as a fellow comrade in the fight of faith, appealing to them to stop speaking curses with their *mouths.*

The word "mouth" is the Greek word *stoma,* which describes *the physical mouth,* but when used figuratively, this is the same term for *the point of a sword.* If you think about it, a knife in the hands of a caring surgeon can heal and save someone's life. On the other hand, that same knife could also be used to damage and destroy someone's life. It all depends on how the knife is used.

The same thing is true of our tongue. We can submit it to the Holy Spirit and speak words of life, or we can use it to speak words of death and destruction. The choice is ours.

Both Sweet and Bitter Often Flow From the Fountain of Our Lips

At this point, James asks a rhetorical question: "Doth a fountain send forth at the same place sweet water and bitter?" (James 3:11) The word "fountain" here is the Greek word *pege*, which indicates that *the mouth is a fountain for what is inside a person* — it is an *outlet* to "send forth" what is in us to others. The Greek word for "send forth" is *bruo*, which means *gush* or *to be gushing forth, like a strong flowing underground stream*.

James said our mouth is like a fountain gushing with "sweet water and bitter." In Greek, this phrase is *to gluku kai to pikron*. The word *glukus* means *sweet*, and the word *pikros* means *acidic, bitter, distasteful, sharp*, or *toxic*. The fact is, natural springs found in the earth don't gush forth with both fresh and bitter water. They yield either one or the other.

Likewise, our mouth should not be a source of both sweet blessings and bitter curses. This is the point James was making, which is why he asked this second rhetorical question: "Can the fig tree, my brethren, bear olive berries? either a vine, figs? so can no fountain both yield salt water and fresh" (James 3:12).

The Evidence of Godly Wisdom Is Proven By the Way We Live

The questions continued as James challenged his readers, saying, "Who is a wise man and endued with knowledge among you? let him shew out of a good conversation his works with meekness of wisdom" (James 3:13). The word "wise" here is the Greek word *sophos*, which was used to portray *highly educated people, such as scientists, philosophers, doctors, teachers, and others who were considered to be the super-intelligentsia of the day*. James uses this term because he is still speaking to any individual who claims to be a masterful teacher of Scripture (a *didaskalos*).

To those who claimed to be a revelator of God's Word, James said, "…Let him shew out of a good conversation his works with meekness of wisdom." The word "shew" here in Greek is *deiknumi*, which describes *something outwardly seen* or *something done visibly to authenticate, prove, or guarantee*. It means *to prove by showing; to display or show off;* or *to demonstrate*.

Basically, James said, "If you really have heavenly wisdom, prove it out of a good conversation." This word "conversation" is the Greek word *anastrophe*, and it describes *a person's conduct* and *verbal conversation*. In a literal sense, the word *anastrophe* here means *a person's rising up, sitting down, going in, and going out*. It is *one's total lifestyle*.

James said, "If you're really moving in the Spirit and speaking heavenly wisdom, prove it by the way you speak and live your life." One of the greatest indicators that God is the source of what a person is saying is the manifestation of meekness marked by wisdom. The Greek word for "meekness" is *prautes*, and it depicts *the attitude or demeanor of a person who is forbearing, patient, and slow to respond in anger*. In a medical sense, this word denotes *soothing medication to calm an angry mind*. Hence, when true, godly wisdom and revelation is being imparted, it is like *soothing medication for an angry soul or for a troubling situation*.

In our next lesson, we'll take a look at what the Bible says about the evidence of wrong revelation.

STUDY QUESTIONS

Study to shew thyself approved unto God, a workman that needeth not to be ashamed, rightly dividing the word of truth.
— 2 Timothy 2:15

As we noted in our last lesson, Scripture is peppered with passages about our speech. Take a few moments to reflect on these verses and write down what the Holy Spirit is showing you in each one.

1. What's the difference between the *mouth of the righteous* and the *mouth of fools*? (*See* Psalm 37:30,31; Proverbs 10:11,13,20,21,31,32.)

2. What kinds of words does God want flowing from our lips? Why? (*See* Proverbs 15:1; 16:24; Ecclesiastes 9:17; Ephesians 4:29-32.)

3. What does God think of murmuring and complaining? (*See* Numbers 21:4-6; 1 Corinthians 10:10,11; Philippians 2:14.)

4. What promise does God make to those who regularly and diligently spend time with Him? (*See* Isaiah 50:4,5.)

PRACTICAL APPLICATION

> **But be ye doers of the word, and not hearers only,
> deceiving your own selves**
> — James 1:22

1. What is your greatest takeaway from this lesson about the tongue being like a poisonous snake ready to pounce and inject its deadly venom into people?

2. Have you ever found yourself in a heated conversation and thought, *Man, I want to give this person a piece of my mind! But I know I shouldn't?* Then no matter how hard you tried to be silent, you eventually exploded with words that cut the other person to pieces? After your emotions settled, were you shocked by what you said and embarrassed by your behavior? Did you ever ask the person to forgive you? How did you make peace?

3. Has anyone ever verbally attacked you? What poisonous words did they speak and release into your life? Take time now to open your heart and invite the healing power of the Holy Spirit in to extract the enemy's venom and restore your soul.

LESSON 4

TOPIC
The Evidence of Wrong Revelation

SCRIPTURES

1. James 3:13-16 — Who is a wise man and endued with knowledge among you? let him shew out of a good conversation his works with meekness of wisdom. But if ye have bitter envying and strife in your hearts, glory not, and lie not against the truth. This wisdom descendeth not from above, but is earthly, sensual, devilish. For where envying and strife is, there is confusion and every evil work.

2. 1 Corinthians 1:10-12 — Now I beseech you, brethren, by the name of our Lord Jesus Christ, that ye all speak the same thing, and that there be no divisions among you; but that ye be perfectly joined together in the same mind and in the same judgment. For it hath been declared unto me of you, my brethren, by them which are of the house of Chloe, that there are contentions among you. Now this I say, that every one of you saith, I am of Paul; and I of Apollos; and I of Cephas; and I of Christ.

GREEK WORDS

1. "wise man" — **σοφὸς** (*sophos*): used to portray highly educated people, such as scientists, philosophers, doctors, teachers, and others who were considered to be the super-intelligentsia of the day; a term reserved only for those considered to be a cut above the rest; insight, revelation, or wisdom not attained by life, experience, or by education; divinely bestowed wisdom

2. "endued with knowledge" — **ἐπιστήμων** (*epistemon*): an expert; one highly skilled; one who is highly enlightened; highly intelligent

3. "shew" — **δείκνυμι** (*deiknumi*): something outwardly seen; something done visibly to authenticate, prove, or guarantee; to prove by showing; to display or show off; to demonstrate

4. "out of a good conversation" — **ἐκ τῆς καλῆς ἀναστροφῆς** (*ek tes kales anastrophes*): the word **ἐκ** (*ek*) means out, **καλός** (*kalos*) and means beautiful, noble, honorable, and **ἀναστροφή** (*anastrophe*) is one's lifestyle or his rising up and setting down, his going in and going out; one's total life that is lived in a noble manner

5. "meekness" — **πραΰτης** (*prautes*): the demeanor of a person who is soothing medication for a troublesome situation or an angry mind or upset soul; denotes the attitude and behavior of one who is warm, patient, kind, and gentle

6. "wisdom" — **σοφία** (*sophia*): wisdom; insight not naturally attained; revelation

7. "have" — **ἔχω** (*echo*): have, hold, or possess; have in possession

8. "bitter" — **πικρία** (*pikria*): inner poison that causes one to eventually become unkind, sour, sharp, sarcastic, scornful, cynical, mocking, contemptuous, and wounding

9. "envying" — ζῆλος (*zelos*): a self-consumed person who is driven to see his agenda adopted; one who is competitive; denotes one upset because someone else achieved more or received more; one who is jealous, envious, resentful, and filled with ill will for the one who got what he wanted; irritated, infuriated, irate, annoyed, provoked, and fuming; one who is incensed

10. "strife" — ἐριθεία (*eritheia*): a political party; often translated "a party spirit" because of its connection to political systems and political parties; pictures individuals or groups of people who push their agenda and ideas, fighting fiercely to see their platform accepted; self-seeking ambition that is more concerned about itself and the fulfillment of its own wants, desires, and pleasures than it is in meeting the needs in others; pictures one so bent on getting what he wants that he is willing to do anything, say anything, and sacrifice any standard, rules, or relationship to achieve his goals; a selfish, self-focused attitude that is engrossed with its own desires and ambitions; one so self-consumed that he is blinded to the desires or ambitions of others; pictures a person who is jockeying for some kind of position

11. "in your hearts" — ἐν τῇ καρδίᾳ ὑμῶν (*n te kardia humon*): literally, in your hearts; indicating this is a heart issue

12. "glory" — κατακαυχάομαι (*katakauchaomai*): over-exalting at the expense of another; actions that exalt one and downgrade another

13. "lie" — ψεύδομαι (*pseudomai*): one who walks in a pretense that is untrue; who intentionally misrepresents facts or truths

14. "wisdom" — σοφία (*sophia*): wisdom; insight not naturally attained; revelation

15. "descendeth" — κατέρχομαι (*katerchomai*): literally, does not come down; descend

16. "from above" — ἄνωθεν (*anothen*): from above; meaning, from a heavenly source

17. "earthly" — ἐπίγειος (*epigeios*): from the earth; right from the earth; referring to the earth realm

18. "sensual" — ψυχικός (*psuchikos*): soulish; belonging to the soulish realm

19. "devilish" — δαιμονιώδης (*daimoniodes*): demonic; demon-like; influenced by demons

20. "confusion" — ἀκαταστασία (*akatastasia*): anarchy, chaos, insubordination

21. "evil" — **φαῦλος** (*phaulos*): something that stinks; something that is rotting, such as meat full of maggots; dead, decaying, and stinking

22. "work" — **πρᾶγμα** (*pragma*): deed; action; also connected to occultic activity

SYNOPSIS

Are you beginning to see how powerful your words are? They are either constructive or destructive. They can either produce life and healing or bring death and destruction. It is our words that reveal our true level of spiritual maturity and determine what fills our hearts. Jesus made this crystal clear:

> **A good man out of the good treasure of his heart brings forth good; and an evil man out of the evil treasure of his heart brings forth evil. For out of the abundance of the heart his mouth speaks.**
>
> **— Luke 6:45 (*NKJV*)**

It is the quality of our words along with our attitudes and actions that determines whether or not we are speaking divine wisdom from Heaven or if we are merely mouthing the fleshly wisdom of man.

The emphasis of this lesson:

A great indicator that God is the source of the revelation being spoken is the display of meekness in the speaker. The absence of meekness and the presence of bitter envy, strife, and self-exaltation are all signs of ungodly revelation that is earthly, sensual, and devilish. When true, godly wisdom and revelation are being imparted, it is like soothing medication for one who is troubled.

A Review of Our Anchor Verse

Looking once more at James 3:1, it says, "My brethren, be not many masters, knowing that we shall receive the greater condemnation." In this verse, James is speaking to anyone who aspires to be a teacher of Scripture. We have seen that the word "masters" is the Greek word *didaskalos*, which describes a *masterful teacher* or *one who has a masterful grip on the Scriptures*. It's the Greek equivalent for the Hebrew word *Rabbi*.

The word *didaskalos* is the very same word used throughout the four gospels by the disciples when they called Jesus "Master." In the context of James 3:1, this word is used to caution us not to be too hasty to claim to be masterful teachers because they "…shall receive the greater condemnation."

We learned that the word "condemnation" in Greek is *krima*, which is from the word *krino*, and is basically *a final verdict handed down by a court of law*. In this case, Heaven is the courtroom and God Himself is the Judge. James is telling us that anyone who claims to be a teacher of God's Word and speaks in a public forum will be scrutinized by God Himself. He will watch and listen to every word and phrase being spoken to determine whether or not that person is truly a *didaskalos* — a masterful teacher.

Friend, if you say you're a teacher of Scripture, God is watching you closely. He is concerned with what is taught in a public forum in His Name and on His behalf. In fact, the only person you should ever be concerned about pleasing is God, because He is the One who will hand down the final verdict, declaring whether or not you are truly His mouthpiece.

Unpreparedness in Teaching Leads to Doctrinal Error

The truth is many people who teach the Word innocently make mistakes at times. This is what we saw happening at the church in Ephesus in Lesson 1. Paul wrote to Timothy about some of the Ephesian believers and said they were "desiring to be teachers of the law; [but] understanding neither what they say, nor whereof they affirm" (1 Timothy 1:7).

The word "desiring" in Greek is the word *thelo*, and here it describes *an earnest, ongoing, perpetual desire or longing*. Paul noted that a number of the Ephesian believers were *longing* to be "teachers of the law," which is a translation of the Greek word *nomodidaskalos*, a word that only appears three times in the New Testament, and it pictures *a scripture-lawyer or someone scholarly in interpreting the Bible*.

Paul's words to Timothy seem to indicate that those who longed to be and claimed to be masterful teachers of God's Word were not ready to teach in a public setting. They may have been greatly gifted and filled with deep desire to teach, but they were unqualified. That is why Paul said, "…[They were] understanding neither what they say, nor whereof they affirm" (1 Timothy 1:7).

The word "understanding" in Greek is *noountes*, a form of the word *nous*, which is the word for *the mind*. Here it refers to *the ability to think, to reason, to understand, and to comprehend*. The use of this word here indicates that these believers who were claiming to be masterful teachers only had a minimal understanding of a few fragments of Scripture. Therefore, they were unable to see and accurately grasp the big picture. As a result, they were teaching doctrinal error.

Think about it. If you needed an operation — such as a heart or kidney transplant — you would want someone who was extremely knowledgeable, highly-skilled, and had years of experience to perform the surgery. In the same way, when a teacher of God's Word is operating on your soul and spirit, you want them to really know the Word so they can accurately apply it to your life. That is what is needed to produce optimal spiritual health.

One's Total Lifestyle Confirms or Disproves His Claim To Be a Revelator of Truth

It is at this point James challenged his readers by saying, "Who is a wise man and endued with knowledge among you? let him shew out of a good conversation his works with meekness of wisdom" (James 3:13). The word "wise" here is the Greek word *sophos*, which was used to portray *highly educated people, such as scientists, philosophers, doctors, teachers, and others who were considered to be the super-intelligentsia of the day*.

The phrase "endued with knowledge" is a translation of the Greek word *epistemon*, which describes *an expert; one highly skilled; one who is highly enlightened*; and *one highly intelligent*. James used this term because he was speaking to any individual who claimed to be endued with divine knowledge of Scripture.

To those who say they are a revelator of God's Word, James advised, "…Let him shew out of a good conversation his works with meekness of wisdom" (James 3:13). The word "shew" here in Greek is *deiknumi*, which describes *something outwardly seen* or *something done visibly to authenticate, prove, or guarantee*. It means *to prove by showing; to display or show off*; or *to demonstrate*.

Basically, James said, "If you really have heavenly wisdom from above, prove it." In particular, he said, "…Shew [it] out of a good conversation…" (James 3:13). In Greek, the word "good" is *kalos*, and it means *beautiful*, *noble*, or *honorable*. The word "conversation" is the Greek word *anastrophes*, and it describes *a person's conduct* and *verbal conversation*. In a literal sense, the word *anastrophes* here denotes *a person's rising up, their sitting down, their going in, and their going out*. It is *one's total lifestyle*.

Thus, James said, "If you're really moving in the Spirit and speaking heavenly wisdom, authenticate it by the noble way you speak and live your life." One of the greatest indicators that God is the source of what a person is speaking is the manifestation of *meekness* marked by wisdom. The Greek word for "meekness" is *prautes*, and it depicts *the attitude of a person who is forbearing, patient, and slow to anger*. This word was used in a medical sense to denote *soothing medication to calm a troubled or angry mind*. Hence, when true, godly wisdom and revelation are being imparted, it is like *soothing medication for one who is troubled*.

Real heavenly revelation never forces itself on anyone.

A Vivid Picture of Bitter-Envy and Strife

James continued his candid instructions by saying, But if ye have bitter envying and strife in your hearts, glory not, and lie not against the truth" (James 3:14). The word "have" is a form of the Greek word *echo*, meaning *to have, to hold, to possess*, or *to have in one's possession*. James said, "If you have in your possession bitter envying and strife in your hearts…." Notice the location of the problem: *in your hearts*. Bitter envy and strife are a heart issue.

The word "bitter" here is the Greek word *pikria*, which denotes *an inner poison that causes one to eventually become unkind, sour, sharp, sarcastic, scornful, cynical, mocking, contemptuous, and wounding with his words*. The word "envying" in Greek is a translation of the word *zelos*, and it depicts *a self-consumed person who is driven to see his agenda adopted*. It is *one who is competitive* and denotes *one who is upset because someone else achieved more or received more*. A person who is "envying" is *one who is jealous, envious, resentful, and filled with ill will for the one who got what he wanted*. This word carries the idea of being *irritated, infuriated, irate, annoyed, provoked, and fuming; one who is incensed about something*.

In addition to having bitter envying in their hearts, James also noted some of his readers were filled with "strife." In Greek, this is the word *eritheia*, which is the First Century term to describe *a political party* and is often translated "a party spirit" because of its connection to political systems and political parties. This word pictures *individuals or groups of people who push their agenda and ideas, fighting fiercely to see their platform accepted.* It is *a self-seeking ambition that is more concerned about itself and the fulfillment of its own wants, desires, and pleasures than it is in meeting the needs of others.*

Moreover, this word *eritheia* — translated here as "strife" — pictures one so bent on getting what he wants that he is willing to do anything, say anything, and sacrifice any standard, rule, or relationship to achieve his goals. It is *a selfish, self-focused attitude that is engrossed with its own desires and ambitions; one so self-consumed that he is blinded to the desires or ambitions of others.* It depicts a person who is jockeying for some kind of position.

The Corinthian Church Was Embroiled in a Civil War

Interestingly, the apostle Paul used this word *eritheia* in his first letter to the Corinthians. He wrote, "Now I beseech you, brethren, by the name of our Lord Jesus Christ, that ye all speak the same thing, and that there be no divisions among you; but that ye be perfectly joined together in the same mind and in the same judgment" (1 Corinthians 1:10).

In Greek, the phrase "perfectly joined together" describes *a time of restoration after a civil war.* It is a time of peace and civility after brothers have fought brothers and families have fought families; when weapons are put away and restoration and order are restored. Paul's use of this word tells us that the kind of fight going on inside the church of Corinth was like a civil war.

When we come to verse 11, we learn more of the details of what was happening. Paul said, "For it hath been declared unto me of you, my brethren, by them which are of the house of Chloe, that there are *contentions* among you." This word "contentions" is *eritheia* — the same Greek word translated as "strife" in James 3:14. Again, it is the word for *a political party* and depicts *individuals or groups of people who push their agenda and ideas, fighting fiercely to see their platform accepted.*

In an effort to squash the civil war in the Corinthian church, Paul said, "Now this I say, that every one of you saith, I am of Paul; and I of Apollos; and I of Cephas; and I of Christ. Is Christ divided?..." (1 Corinthians 1:12,13). Clearly, the church of Corinth had divided into political parties. Although political parties are acceptable in a democracy, they are unacceptable for any church in any age.

Wherever a spirit of strife — *eritheia* — is at work, it is not of God, and it is evidence that whatever is being promoted did not come from Heaven.

Ungodly Wisdom Exalts Itself and Downgrades Others

Looking once more at James 3:14, it says, "But if ye have bitter envying and strife in your hearts, glory not, and lie not against the truth." In Greek, the words "glory not" mean *don't over-exalt at the expense of another — don't act in ways that exalt one and downgrade another.* If you're exalting yourself in the name of revelation and simultaneously downgrading someone else, that is not the behavior of God, and therefore, it is not the wisdom of God. It fails the test.

James also said, "...Lie not against the truth" (James 3:14). The word "lie" here is the Greek word *pseudomai*, which describes *one who walks in a pretense that is untrue* or *one who intentionally misrepresents facts or truths.* Many times those who claim to be moving in divine revelation think they have the right to behave inappropriately, but that is not true.

We learn from James in verse 15, "This wisdom descendeth not from above, but is earthly, sensual, devilish" (James 3:15). The word "wisdom" here is the Greek word *sophia*, which describes *wisdom, revelation,* or *insight not naturally attained.* In this instance, it is *any so-called wisdom that is tainted with bitter envy, strife, selfish ambition, and self-exaltation.* James said this kind of wisdom "...descendeth not from above..." (James 3:15).

The phrase "descendeth not" in Greek is from the word *katerchomai,* and it literally means *does not come down* or *descend.* The words "from above" is a translation of the Greek word *anothen,* meaning *from above* or *from a heavenly source.* James said this twisted kind of wisdom is "...earthly, sensual, devilish" (James 3:15).

Ungodly Wisdom Is
'Earthly, Sensual, and Devilish'

The word "earthly" is the Greek word *epigeios*, which means *from the earth; right from the earth*; or *referring to the earth realm*. The word "sensual" in Greek is *psuchikos*, and it means *soulish* or *belonging to the soulish realm*. Many times people are moving in the soulish dimension — operating out of their mind, will and emotions — and they mistake what they're sensing as something of the Spirit, but it is not. Demons operate in the realm of the soul, which is why James tells us that this perverted type of wisdom is "devilish." In Greek, the word "devilish" is *daimoniodes*, which describes *something demonic; demon-like*; or *influenced by demons*.

To make sure we comprehend what ungodly wisdom looks like, James tells us point blank, "For where envying and strife is, there is confusion and every evil work" (James 3:16). Again, we see the word *zelos*, translated as "envying," and the word *eritheia*, translated as "strife" — the same two words that appear in James 3:14. Remember, "envying" is *a fierce desire to promote your own ideas and your own beliefs to the exclusion of everyone else*, and "strife" is a "party-spirit" that seeks to divide up into political parties and go to war and build factions inside the Church.

What other indicators of ungodly wisdom does James give us? He says, "...[Where] there is confusion and every evil work" (James 3:16). The word "confusion" is the Greek word *akatastasia*, which describes *anarchy, chaos*, and *insubordination*. The word "evil" in Greek is *phaulos*, which denotes *something that stinks* or *something that is rotting*, such as maggot-infested meat. Hence, ungodly revelation is *dead, decaying*, and *stinking*, and there is no life of God in it. Finally, we have the word "work" — the Greek word *pragma*, which describes *a deed* or *an action*. It is the very same word used to describe *occult activity* or *witchcraft*.

Thus, any manipulation or attempts to control people and situations — even in the name of "divine" revelation — is not of God. It is ungodly wisdom that is earthly, sensual, and downright devilish.

Taking into account the original Greek meaning of these key words, here is the *Renner Interpretive Version (RIV)* of James 3:14 and 15:

> **If you have an attitude that makes you sarcastic, cynical, mocking, contemptuous, and wounding of others; if you're driven to**

see your view or agenda adopted at the expense of others, and if you are irritated, infuriated, irate, annoyed, provoked, fuming or incensed with others and so filled with strife inside your heart that you're blinded to the desires or needs of others — if you are jockeying for advantage even if it is to the disadvantage of others — then stop these actions and attitudes that are being carried out at the expense of others and quit projecting yourself as doing it all with right motives, because it isn't true.

This is emphatically not the wisdom that comes down from Heaven, but on the contrary, it emphatically is from a low-level earthly realm. It is pure soulish activity, and anyone who is thinking and behaving like this is clearly under the influence of demonic activity.

In our fifth and final lesson, we will focus on the evidence of real, heavenly revelation that is from above.

STUDY QUESTIONS

> Study to shew thyself approved unto God, a workman that
> needeth not to be ashamed, rightly dividing the word of truth.
> — 2 Timothy 2:15

1. Self-promotion and self-exaltation is a sure sign of earthly, sensual, ungodly wisdom. What instruction does Paul offer in Romans 12:3 and Philippians 2:1-4 that helps us curb our tendency to be self-focused?

2. According to Philippians 2:5-8, what attitude should we pray for the Holy Spirit to cultivate in us and what could the evidence of this trait look like in your life?

3. "Meekness" is the mark of spiritual maturity and heavenly wisdom. It is *the attitude of patience, self-control, and being slow to anger.* In a medical sense, it denotes *soothing medication to calm a troubled or angry mind.* What did Jesus invite us to do in Matthew 11:28-30 that will help us develop meekness in our lives?

PRACTICAL APPLICATION

But be ye doers of the word, and not hearers only,
deceiving your own selves.
— James 1:22

1. Imagine you need a life-or-death surgery, like a heart or kidney transplant. Would you want a surgeon who had a strong desire to be a surgeon but only had three months of schooling? Or would you want a surgeon who was extremely knowledgeable, highly skilled, and had years of experience? Once you know your answer, explain how this example also applies to people who teach God's Word.

2. Take time to reread the Greek definitions of the words "bitter" (*pikria*), "envying" (*zelos*), and "strife" (*eritheia*), which are all marks of low-level, fleshly wisdom. Be honest with yourself: Do any of these words describe you? If so, which one (or ones)? Pray and ask the Holy Spirit to show you where and when these attitudes began in your life. Repent, receive His forgiveness, and trust Him to change you.

LESSON 5

TOPIC

The Evidence of Right Revelation

SCRIPTURES

1. James 3:14-18 — But if ye have bitter envying and strife in your hearts, glory not, and lie not against the truth. This wisdom descendeth not from above, but is earthly, sensual, devilish. For where envying and strife is, there is confusion and every evil work. But the wisdom that is from above is first pure, then peaceable, gentle, and easy to be intreated, full of mercy and good fruits, without partiality, and without hypocrisy. And the fruit of righteousness is sown in peace of them that make peace.

GREEK WORDS

1. "have" — ἔχω (*echo*): have, hold, or possess

2. "bitter" — **πικρία** (*pikria*): inner poison that causes one to eventually become unkind, sour, sharp, sarcastic, scornful, cynical, mocking, contemptuous, and wounding

3. "envying" — **ζῆλος** (*zelos*): a self-consumed person who is driven to see his agenda adopted; one who is competitive; denotes one upset because someone else achieved more or received more; one who is jealous, envious, resentful, and filled with ill will for the one who got what he wanted; irritated, infuriated, irate, annoyed, provoked, and fuming; one who is incensed

4. "strife" — **ἐριθεία** (*eritheia*): a political party; often translated "a party spirit" because of its connection to political systems and political parties; pictures individuals or groups of people who push their agenda and ideas, fighting fiercely to see their platform accepted; self-seeking ambition that is more concerned about itself and the fulfillment of its own wants, desires, and pleasures than it is in meeting the needs in others; pictures one so bent on getting what he wants that he is willing to do anything, say anything, and sacrifice any standard, rules, or relationship to achieve his goals; a selfish, self-focused attitude that is engrossed with its own desires and ambitions; one so self-consumed that he is blinded to the desires or ambitions of others; pictures a person who is jockeying for some kind of position

5. "in your hearts" — **ἐν τῇ καρδίᾳ ὑμῶν** (*n te kardia humon*): literally, in your hearts; indicating this is a heart issue

6. "glory" — **κατακαυχάομαι** (*katakauchaomai*): over-exalting at the expense of another; actions that exalt one and downgrade another

7. "lie" — **ψεύδομαι** (*pseudomai*): one who walks in a pretense that is untrue; who intentionally misrepresents facts or truths

8. "wisdom" — **σοφία** (*sophia*): wisdom; insight not naturally attained; revelation

9. "descendeth" — **κατέρχομαι** (*katerchomai*): literally, does not come down; descend

10. "from above" — **ἄνωθεν** (*anothen*): from above; meaning, from a heavenly source

11. "earthly" — **ἐπίγειος** (*epigeios*): from the earth; right from the earth; referring to the earth realm

12. "sensual" — **ψυχικός** (*psuchikos*): soulish; belonging to the soulish realm

13. "devilish" — **δαιμονιώδης** (*daimoniodes*): demonic; demon-like; influenced by demons

14. "where" — **ὅπου** (*hopou*): where; in what place; any place; wherever

15. "confusion" — **ἀκαταστασία** (*akatastasia*): anarchy, chaos, insubordination, or some kind of attitude or action that creates upheaval, unrest, or instability; the attitude or actions of a person who creates some type of disastrous disturbance; any lack of stability, confusion, or anything unstable

16. "every" — **πᾶν** (*pan*): all; an all-inclusive word, leaving nothing out

17. "evil" — **φαῦλος** (*phaulos*): something that stinks; something that is rotting, such as meat full of maggots; dead, decaying, and stinking

18. "work" — **πρᾶγμα** (*pragma*): deed; action; also connected to occultic activity

19. "wisdom" — **σοφία** (*sophia*): wisdom; insight not naturally attained; revelation

20. "from above" — **ἄνωθεν** (*anothen*): from above; meaning, from a heavenly source

21. "first" — **πρῶτον** (*proton*): first and foremost

22. "pure" — **ἁγνός** (*hagnos*): pure inside and out; uncontaminated

23. "peaceable" — **εἰρηνικός** (*eirenikos*): peace-conquering; peace-dominating

24. "gentle" — **ἐπιεικής** (*epieikes*): mild; gentle; soothing medication to angry minds and emotions

25. "easy to be intreated" — **εὐπειθής** (*eupeithes*): pictures one that is reasonable or agreeable, as opposed to one who is ugly and obstinate in his behavior

26. "without hypocrisy" — **ἀνυπόκριτος** (*anupokritos*): authentic, genuine; it is the opposite of something pretended, simulated, faked, feigned, or phony; one who is authentic

SYNOPSIS

In the opening chapter of his first letter to the church at Corinth, the apostle Paul made this powerful statement: "…From this same God you have received your standing in Jesus Christ, and he has become for us the *true wisdom…*" (1 Corinthians 1:30 *Phillips*). Friend, the more and more you come to know Jesus through your daily walk with Him, the more you will come to know and recognize true wisdom. Anything that is not found in His character is not found in wisdom.

Through James, the Holy Spirit gives us some very specific evidence of what real revelation from Heaven looks and sounds like. Now that we have examined the irrefutable characteristics of ungodly, earthly wisdom, let's take time to explore what true wisdom from Heaven is.

The emphasis of this lesson:

True godly wisdom is first and foremost pure, and then it is peaceable — which means it is peace-dominating. It is also gentle, agreeable, and authentic. Likewise, real revelation from Heaven is full of mercy and good fruits and never shows partiality.

A Final Review of Our Anchor Verse

Let's take a final look at James 3:1, which says, "My brethren, be not many masters, knowing that we shall receive the greater condemnation." Here, James addressed any person who wants to be *a masterful teacher* of the Word. That is what the word "masters" — the Greek word *didaskalos* — means. It is the Greek equivalent for the Hebrew word *Rabbi* and describes *one who has a masterful grip on the Scriptures.*

James issued a warning not to be too hasty in claiming to be a masterful teacher because they "…shall receive the greater condemnation" (James 3:1). We saw that the Greek word for "condemnation" is *krima*, which is from the word *krino*, and is basically *a final verdict handed down by a court of law after all the evidence has been seen.* In this case, the court of Heaven is watching and listening, and God Himself is the presiding Judge.

Anyone who claims to be a teacher of God's Word and speaks in a public forum will be analyzed by God Himself. God is concerned with what is taught in a public forum *in His Name* and *on His behalf.* He is the One who will hand down the final verdict, declaring whether or not a person is truly speaking the words of Heaven.

The Proof of Wrong Revelation

In our previous lesson, we examined the telltale signs of ungodly, fleshly wisdom. James said, "But if ye have bitter envying and strife in your hearts, glory not, and lie not against the truth" (James 3:14). Two of the greatest indicators that a person is speaking wrong revelation is the presence of *bitter envying* and *strife*.

The word "have" is a form of the Greek word *echo*, meaning *to have, to hold, to possess*, or *to have in one's possession*. James said, "If you have and hold bitter envying and strife in your hearts, glory not…." Here we see where the problem is lodged: *in the heart*. Bitter envy and strife are heart issues.

The word "bitter" in this verse is the Greek word *pikria*, and it describes *an inner poison that causes one to eventually become unkind, sour, sharp, sarcastic, scornful, cynical, mocking, contemptuous, and wounding with his words*. Anyone who uses their sphere of influence or public platform to be contemptuous and wounding of others is not acting as God would act.

The word "envying" is a translation of the Greek word *zelos*, and it depicts *a self-consumed person who is driven to see his agenda adopted*. It is *one who is competitive* and denotes *one who is upset because someone else achieved more or received more*. He cannot rejoice with anyone else being blessed. Rather, his "envying" makes him *jealous, envious, resentful, and filled with ill will for the one who got what he wanted*. This word *zelos* carries the idea of being *irritated, infuriated, irate, annoyed, provoked, and fuming*. It is *one who is incensed about something*, which is not at all the way heavenly wisdom behaves.

Along with bitter envying, James said "strife" is also characteristic of ungodly wisdom. In Greek, this is the word *eritheia*, which describes *a political party* and is often translated "a party spirit" because of its connection to political systems and political agendas. This word pictures *individuals or groups of people who push their agenda and ideas, fighting fiercely to see their platform adopted*. It is *a self-seeking ambition that is more concerned about itself and the fulfillment of its own wants, desires, and plea-sures than it is in meeting the needs in others*.

Furthermore, this word *eritheia* — translated here as "strife" — pictures *one so bent on getting what he wants that he is willing to do anything, say anything, and sacrifice any standard, rule, or relationship to achieve his goals*. It is *a selfish, self-focused attitude that is so engrossed with its own desires and ambitions* that he is *blinded to the desires or ambitions of others*. This self-consumed person is always jockeying for some kind of position.

Strife and Division Had Spread Throughout the Corinthian Church

What is remarkable about this word *eritheia* — the word for "strife" — is that the apostle Paul used it in his first letter to the Corinthian believers. The reason this seems odd is because the church at Corinth was filled with and flowing in the gifts of the Holy Spirit. In fact, there were so many gifts of the Spirit in operation they couldn't be counted! Yet, Paul wrote them and said, "Now I beseech you, brethren, by the name of our Lord Jesus Christ, that ye all speak the same thing, and that there be no divisions among you; but that ye be perfectly joined together in the same mind and in the same judgment" (1 Corinthians 1:10).

Apparently, the Corinthian believers were not all speaking the same thing and there were obvious divisions among them. That's why Paul told them to be "perfectly joined together." In Greek, this phrase describes *a time of restoration after a civil war, a time of peace and civility after brothers have fought brothers and families have fought families.* It's a time when weapons are put away and restoration and order are restored. Paul's use of this word lets us know the kind of battle that was taking place inside the church of Corinth.

In the very next verse, we discover more specifics of what was happening. Paul said, "For it hath been declared unto me of you, my brethren, by them which are of the house of Chloe, that there are *contentions* among you" (I Corinthians 1:11). The word "contentions" here is the Greek word *eritheia* — the same word translated as "strife" in James 3:14. This tells us there were *individuals or groups of people who were pushing their agenda and ideas, fighting fiercely to see their platform accepted.* Each party in the church believed their "revelation" and style of ministry was more important than everyone else's, and therefore was jockeying for the top position.

In his straightforward way, Paul told the Corinthians, "Now this I say, that every one of you saith, I am of Paul; and I of Apollos; and I of Cephas; and I of Christ. Is Christ divided?" (1 Corinthians 1:12,13) So from this verse we see there was a "Paul party," an "Apollos party," a "Cephas (Peter) party," and a "Christ party." Each group preferred the style and personality of its leader and thought it should be the standard for everyone — so much so that they were fighting over it.

Essentially, Paul said, "Enough! This political infighting is inappropriate in the Church. Stop it. Put away your weapons and be 'perfectly joined together.' Make the decision to restore civility and begin rebuilding and restoring the bond of unity and love among you." Indeed, political parties are acceptable in a democracy, but they are unacceptable for any church in any age. When you see strife (*eritheia*) at work, it is evidence that what is being promoted did not come from God.

True Wisdom From Heaven Never Exalts Itself or Puts Others Down

Returning to our text in James 3:14, it says, "But if ye have bitter envying and strife in your hearts, glory not, and lie not against the truth." When James said "glory not," the Greek he used means *don't over-exalt yourself at the expense of another — don't act in ways that exalt one and downgrade another.* This tells us if we're exalting ourselves and simultaneously putting down someone else in the name of "godly wisdom and revelation," what we're doing is *not* of God.

Additionally, James said, "...Lie not against the truth" (James 3:14). In Greek, the word "lie" here is the word *pseudomai*, which describes *one who walks in a pretense that is untrue* or *one who intentionally misrepresents facts or truths.* This person claims to be moving in the Spirit and speaking divine revelation, and because they're speaking on God's behalf, they claim they have the right to talk about and bash others. But that is not true. God never degrades people nor approves of those who do.

That is why James says in verse 15, "This wisdom descendeth not from above, but is earthly, sensual, devilish" (James 3:15). The word "wisdom" is the Greek word *sophia*, and here it denotes *wisdom, revelation,* or *insight from God* we are asserting to possess. Any so-called wisdom that is tainted with *bitter envy, strife, selfish ambition, and self-exaltation* "...descendeth not from above..." (James 3:15).

In Greek, the phrase "descendeth not" is from the word *katerchomai*, which literally means *does not come down* or *descend.* The words "from above" are a translation of the Greek word *anothen*, meaning *from above* or *from a heavenly source.* Hence, James said this twisted kind of wisdom is "...earthly, sensual, devilish" (James 3:15).

Be Careful Not To Confuse Soulish Desires
For Heavenly Wisdom

Understanding these three words — *earthly, sensual,* and *devilish* — is very important. First, the word "earthly" in Greek is *epigeios*, which means *from the earth; right from the earth*; or *belonging to the earthly realm.*

Second is the word "sensual," which is the Greek word *psuchikos*, and it signifies *something soulish* or *belonging to the soulish realm.* At times our personal desires and emotions about seeing a certain thing take place are so strong we can confuse them for God's voice of direction. The truth is, however, we are merely moving in the soulish dimension — operating out of our mind, will, and emotions — and not hearing from God's Spirit at all.

Keep in mind that the realm of the soul is the place where demons operate, which is why James told us that any "wisdom" intermingled with bitter envying and strife is "devilish." The word "devilish" in Greek is *daimoniodes*, which means it is *something demonic; demon-like*; or *influenced by demonic activity.*

Taking into account the original Greek meaning of all these key words, here is the *Renner Interpretive Version (RIV)* of James 3:14 and 15:

If you have an attitude that makes you sarcastic, cynical, mocking, contemptuous, and wounding of others; if you're driven to see your view or agenda adopted at the expense of others, and if you are irritated, infuriated, irate, annoyed, provoked, fuming or incensed with others and so filled with strife inside your heart that you're blinded to the desires or needs of others — if you are jockeying for advantage even if it is to the disadvantage of others — then stop these actions and attitudes that are being carried out at the expense of others and quit projecting yourself as doing it all with right motives, because it isn't true.

This is emphatically not the wisdom that comes down from Heaven, but on the contrary, it emphatically is from a low-level earthly realm. It is pure soulish activity, and anyone who is thinking and behaving like this is clearly under the influence of demonic activity

Where Envy and Strife Are Operating
There Is 'Confusion and Every Evil Work'

To make certain we get a clear picture of what ungodly wisdom looks like, James put it bluntly, "For where envying and strife is, there is confusion and every evil work" (James 3:16). Again, we see the words "envying and strife." The word "envying" is the word *zelos*, and the word "strife" is the word *eritheia*, the same two words appearing in James 3:14. Remember, "envying" is a fierce desire to promote your own ideas and your own beliefs to the exclusion of everyone else; and "strife" is a "party-spirit" that seeks to divide up into political parties, go to war, and build factions inside the Church.

When envying and strife are at work, James said, "...There is confusion and every evil work" (James 3:16). The word "confusion" is the Greek word *akatastasia*, which describes *anarchy, chaos,* and *insubordination.* It is some kind of attitude or action that creates upheaval, unrest, or instability.

This brings us to the phrase "every evil work." The word "every" in Greek is *pan*, which is an all-inclusive word, meaning *all, leaving nothing out.* The word "evil" is the Greek word *phaulos*, which denotes *something that stinks* or *something that is rotting*, such as meat that is full of maggots. Hence, ungodly revelation is *dead, decaying,* and *stinking,* and totally void of the life of God.

Finally, we have the word "work" — the Greek word *pragma* — which describes *an activity, a deed,* or *an action.* Interestingly, it is the very same word used in Greek literature to describe *occult activity* or *witchcraft.* Thus, any manipulation or attempt to control people and situations — even in the name of "divine" revelation — is not of God. It is ungodly wisdom that is earthly, sensual, and downright devilish.

What Does Godly Wisdom Look Like?

After vividly painting the picture of what low-level, ungodly wisdom looks like, James declared, "But the wisdom that is from above is first pure, then peaceable, gentle, and easy to be intreated, full of mercy and good fruits, without partiality, and without hypocrisy" (James 3:17). Like all the verses before it, this one contains many important words we need to understand.

First, note the word "wisdom." Again, it is the Greek word *sophia*, which describes *wisdom* and *insight not naturally attained*. In context here, this is *supernaturally imparted revelation* "from above." In Greek, the words "from above" are a translation of the word *anothen*, meaning *from above* or *from a heavenly source*.

Real heavenly revelation from above is "...first pure, then peaceable..." (James 3:17). The word "first" is the Greek word *proton*, which means *first and foremost*. The word "pure" in Greek is *hagnos*, signifying *something pure inside and out* or *something uncontaminated*. And the word "peaceable" is a compound of the words *eirene* and *nikos*. The word *eirene* is the word for *peace* and describes *the cessation of war and a time of civility and rebuilding*. The word *nikos* means *to conquer*. When these words are compounded to form the new word *eirenikos*, translated "peaceable," it means *peace-conquering* or *peace-dominating*.

When wisdom and revelation really come from Heaven, it comes with a sense of dominating peace. There is no strife, no arguing, no manipulation, and no self-exaltation involved. Only God's fingerprints of peace can be found and felt.

Real heavenly revelation from above is also "...gentle, and easy to be intreated, full of mercy and good fruits, without partiality, and without hypocrisy" (James 3:17).

Notice the word "gentle" here. It is the Greek word *epieikes*, which means *mild* or *gentle*. It is like *soothing medication to angry minds and emotions*. Thus, when real heavenly wisdom comes, it is like medication to the soul, bringing comfort, encouragement, and healing.

Wisdom from above is also "easy to be intreated." This phrase is a translation of the Greek word *eupeithes*, which pictures *a person that is reasonable or agreeable, as opposed to one who is ugly and obstinate in his behavior*. In other words, godly wisdom is not harsh, demanding, or stubborn. It is also "without hypocrisy," which in the Greek means *authentic* and *genuine*. It is *the opposite of something pretended, simulated, faked, feigned, or phony*. It is *one who is authentic.*

James concludes his teaching on how to recognize godly wisdom by saying, "And the fruit of righteousness is sown in peace of them that make peace" (James 3:18). Again, we see this direct connection between peace and genuine revelation from above. This tells us that real heavenly wisdom always makes peace — hence, it is peace-conquering and peace-dominating.

Taking into account the original Greek meaning of all these key words, here is the *Renner Interpretive Version (RIV)* of James 3:17:

> **Wisdom that comes from a heavenly source is first of all recognizable because of its impeccable behavior. It comes with a dominating sense of peace and is characterized by a mild, kind, temperate, calm, and gentle behavior that comforts, calms, softens, and brings healing to others. Real heavenly wisdom gets along easily with others and never demands its own way with ugly and unreasonable behavior. It is filled to the brim with so much compassion that it finds a way to be helpful in any way possible. Such wisdom does not practice favoritism. It is authentic and genuine.**

Friend, God's wisdom is extravagantly wonderful! It brings solutions to problems and answers to long-held questions. God wants you to know and recognize His voice of wisdom speaking through others, and at the same time wants to prepare you to share His revelation with others. Take time to work through the Study and Application Questions, and allow the Holy Spirit to seal the truths of these teachings deep within your heart!

STUDY QUESTIONS

> **Study to shew thyself approved unto God, a workman that needeth not to be ashamed, rightly dividing the word of truth.**
> **— 2 Timothy 2:15**

1. Read back through the *RIV* of James 3:17. Does this description of godly wisdom remind you of another passage? Hint: check out First Corinthians 13:4-8. What similarities do you see between the two?

2. Knowing that God is love (*see* 1 John 4:8,16), and wisdom that's truly from Him is consistent with His character, how does this help you determine what godly wisdom from others will sound like — and what it won't sound like?

3. Moving forward, what steps can you take to recognize and guard your heart and mind from counterfeit wisdom that is earthly, soulish, and devilish? (Consider committing to memory James 3:17 along with Paul's words in Philippians 4:8.)

PRACTICAL APPLICATION

But be ye doers of the word, and not hearers only,
deceiving your own selves.
— James 1:22

1. When you're really living by the Spirit and speaking heavenly wisdom, what you say and the way you live will prove it. Be honest: What do your *attitudes*, *actions*, and *words* say about you? If your closest friends were to answer this question, how do you think they'd respond? Where do you need help to come up higher and live more like Jesus? Take a few moments to pray, surrender yourself — struggles and all — to God and invite His Spirit to mature you.

2. Take time to reflect on the meanings of the words "peaceable," "gentle," and "easy to be entreated." Using these definitions as a criterion for true, godly wisdom, what have you heard or been listening to — in the news, from friends, or even in the form of Christian teaching — that you can now see doesn't measure up to God's standard?

3. Friend, God loves you so much! And He wants to help you tame your tongue and learn how to recognize real, heavenly revelation from Him. Take a moment now to pray this prayer from your heart:

   Father, thank You for the powerful truths You've shown me in these teachings. Please forgive me for ever using my mouth in hurtful ways and for operating in bitter envying and strife at times. I surrender myself to You anew right now. Take my mouth and purify it — make it a true fountain of life full of blessings and void of curses. Sanctify my soul — my thinking, my feelings, and my decision making — and bring it into total alignment with Your will (see 1 Thessalonians 5:23,24). Holy Spirit, lead me daily and show me my part in seeing this prayer answered. In the mighty name of Jesus. Amen!

Notes

www.ingramcontent.com/pod-product-compliance
Lightning Source LLC
Chambersburg PA
CBHW051047030426

42339CB00006B/241